编委会

主　　任　李学通

编委会委员　卞修跃　古为明　刘　萍　李学通　张会芳
　　　　　　　吴胜利　程朝云　徐　宏　鲍　宁　詹利萍

西方的中国影像
1793—1949

亚瑟·威廉·佩奈尔卷 （一）

主编 卞修跃 ｜ 本卷主编 卞修跃

黄山书社

图书在版编目（CIP）数据

西方的中国影像（1793—1949）亚瑟·威廉·佩奈尔卷 / 卞修跃主编 .—合肥：黄山书社，2015.1

ISBN 978-7-5461-4909-7

Ⅰ．①西… Ⅱ．①卞… Ⅲ．①中国历史—1793—1949—图集 Ⅳ．① K250.6-64

中国版本图书馆 CIP 数据核字（2015）第 007313 号

西方的中国影像（1793—1949）
XIFANG DE ZHONGGUO YINGXIANG

| 亚瑟·威廉·佩奈尔卷

出 品 人：任耕耘
总 策 划：任耕耘　郭　京
执行策划：汤吟菲
编辑统筹：徐娟娟
责任编辑：徐娟娟　王舒彦
翻　　译：谈　杨
责任印制：戚　帅
装帧设计：未　泯　王路漫　刘　俊
排　　版：安徽奇景文化传媒有限责任公司

出版发行：时代出版传媒股份有限公司（http://www.press-mart.com）
　　　　　黄山书社（http://www.hspress.cn/index.asp）
　　　　　（合肥市蜀山区翡翠路1118号出版传媒广场7层　邮编：230071）
经　　销：新华书店
印　　刷：安徽新华印刷股份有限公司
开　　本：889×1194　1/16
印　　张：24.25
版　　次：2015年9月第1版　2015年9月第1次印刷
书　　号：ISBN 978-7-5461-4909-7
定　　价：2400.00元（全二册）

服务热线 0551-63533706
销售热线 0551-63533761
官方直营书店（http://hsssbook.taobao.com）

版权所有　侵权必究
凡本社图书出现印装质量问题，请与印制科联系。
联系电话 0551-63533725

永恒的"瞬间"连缀可见的历史

"第三只眼"中的近世中国(代序)

卞修跃

一

以图记事是人类古老的文化活动之一,是人类的精神本能。

然而,众所周知,在作为中国古代传统正史的二十四史中,图像内容并未被收载。道理其实很简单:在造纸术发明之前,中国的图书镌刻在狭长的木简上,结简成卷;而幅面较大、内容丰富的图像无法在木简这样狭小的介质上存在。此后造纸术和刻版印刷术发明,但同样由于印刷技术的局限,中国传统图书中难以大量用图,这种情况延续了千年之久。

不过,尽管二十四史没有收图入史,但在中国数千年的传统文化之中,从未忽略图形、图像传递信息、传承文化的价值与作用。大而言之,绘影成形,利用图像的形式展现人类认识客观世界、体现人类自身精神生活,几乎是人类与生俱来的精神本能,也是人类最古老的文化活动之一。当人类通过用手劳动,站立起身躯,进化了大脑,产生了精神意识之际,人类便开始认识到自身作为自然界最具特色的存在。他们进行物质生产、生活的同时,智力水平日益提高,精神生活由简单走向复杂。于是,他们在从事原始采集、狩猎的同时,开始逐步认识自己赖以生存的客观世界,并由此逐渐走向对自己精神世界的认识。为了体现这种认识,传承所积累的知识,原始先民们往往会利用天然的、简单的颜料,在岩壁之上、器物之表,或绘,或凿,或铸,刻画出各种人物、动物图案,反映自己的采集、狩猎等现实生活或生殖崇拜等意识观念。如广泛分布于中国西南、东北、西北等地的岩画,黄河流域仰韶文化遗存中画在陶器上的人面、鱼身图案等,都向后世形象生动地展现了这一点。

相对于抽象的文字表述,图形、图像更能生动、形象地反映人们对外部世界的认识,表现日常的生产、生活,展示人类精神生活。因此,即便是在文字发明之后,图形、图像的这种价值也并未削弱。许慎《说文解字·序》称:"黄帝之史仓颉,见鸟兽蹄迒之迹,知分理之可相别异也,初造书契。"虽类属传说,但也从一个方面说明,抽象文字之发生实源自形象的鸟兽之迹,也就是从形象的图案图形中演变进化而来。而在纯粹以文字记载的中国古史中，关于以图记事、以图载史的内容同样不绝如缕。《吴越春秋》称"功可象于图画"。《世本•作篇》曰"史皇作图，仓颉作书"。《吕氏春秋•审分览》载"史皇作图"。《说郛•卷四二》则记："夫画者，肇自伏牺画卦。至黄帝时，史皇、仓颉生焉。史皇状鱼龙之迹，仓颉因而为字，盖画先而书次之。"《拾遗记》卷一《颛顼》亦云"颛顼生，手有文如龙，亦有玉图之象"。《吕氏春秋•先识览》记桀之将亡，"太史终古出其图法……出奔如商"，"殷内史向挚见纣之愈乱迷惑也，于是载其图法，出亡之周"，"晋太史屠黍见……晋公之骄而无德义也，以其图法归周"。《周易•系辞上》则更有名言："河出图，洛出书，圣人则之。"今本《竹书纪年》更细致："黄帝轩辕五十年秋七月……《龙图》出河，《龟书》出洛，赤文篆字，以授轩辕。"《汉书》记刘邦克秦都城，萧何"收律令图书"。以至于后世史家，更是图、书并重。而章学诚则在《和州志》里批评司马迁"始创十表，后世相承，志表愈繁，图经渐失"，把正史中无图的责任全部推给了太史公。自古以来，中国即把书籍径称"图书"，彰显了中国古代图、书并重的传统，以至于后世往往把语出《新唐书•杨绾传》的"左右图史"一词的本义，从用以形容一个人嗜书好学、藏书丰富，引申为中国古代治史、治学的一种图文并重的传统。

此外，于文字书籍之外独立存在的图像，又与文字并行流传，成为人们再现对外部世界认识和内在精神生活不可或缺的工具与形式。文字之所创制，是从形象的图形、图案中抽象演化而来，自不待言。而流传数千年以至今日能为人们所见的，如商周彝鼎之纹，汉代画像石、画像砖、帛画等物，皆为当时人们对现实生产、生活和精神文化生活的展现，也是今世认识特定历史内容一个重要且形象、生动，弥足珍贵的历史资料。晋唐以降，迄于明清，文明益昌，不同流派的绘画作品汗牛充栋，所反映的内容，更遍及人类社会生活的方方面面。既有纯粹的反映人们衣食住行、重大政治军事活动的纪实作品，如疆域舆图、天文天象、工具制作、生产流程、军事战争、仪典节庆等；也有纯以反映画者内心感受、传达画者精神情感的艺术性绘画，如不同流派的文人画作、山水花鸟鱼虫之类；还有印制在人们生产活动产物上的装饰性图案等，如各类建筑物的雕梁画栋、官民窑瓷上的印花图形、官民服装上的花团锦簇等。

进入近代之后，随着摄影技术的发明（1839年），人们更热衷于把手中的相机，作为观察世界和展现事件进展与社会状况一连串瞬间的"第三只眼"。相机能把人类的眼睛所能看到的一切东西精确、细致地摄制下来，准确地再现，流传至久远，从而为人类更加精确地反映客观世界，乃至凝固稍纵即逝的人类活动瞬间以成永恒画面，提供了强大的、无可匹敌的武器，因此更加丰富了人类以图像记录历史的手段与内容，也为后世留下了取之不尽的影像资料。近年来，随着人们学习与欣赏习惯的变化，历史图像受到社会各界特别是历史学界越来越多的关注和重视，而近代保留下来的无以数计的照片，也同样构成我们这里所说的图像种类之一，成为人们研究历史的最为珍贵的资料。

二

"第三只眼"中的近世中国,形象生动,丰富多彩。

相机是人类认识外部世界的"第三只眼",而近世以来西方世界对中国的观察,同样也是另外一只观察中国的眼睛。近世西方世界对中国的形象认识,大体上是始于1793年英国马戛尔尼使团的随行画家威廉·亚历山大(William Alexander)的画作。当然,此前的中国早已誉满欧洲,"中国热"已经在欧洲持续了很久。从最初听到中国的名字直到启蒙时代,西方世界一向将这个东方古老帝国视为富裕和文明的典范,生起无限的羡慕与神往之情。虽然马戛尔尼一行的来华,没能够完成促使中华帝国打开国门,进而促进对华贸易的使命,使团的随行画家威廉·亚历山大却把他的一路见闻——沿途的风光、庙堂建筑、风俗民情、官员走卒、将军士卒等,绘成画幅,在18、19世纪之交长期成为西方世界对中国最权威,甚至是唯一的形象描述。直到1843年,英国伦敦费舍尔公司出版了一套规模可观的配文画册《中国:那个古老帝国的风景、建筑与社会习俗》(*China: The Scenery, Architecture, and Social Habits of That Ancient Empire*),这一局面才稍有改观。这本由英国建筑师、风景画画家托马斯·阿洛姆(Thomas Allom)精心绘画,历史学家乔治·赖特(George Wright)配文的画册,集当时欧洲中国题材绘画之大成,为西方世界在照相术成熟之前,提供了有关中国社会生活的丰富的历史信息。也正是在这部画册面世之际,英国人在香港岛建起了以女王维多利亚名字命名的港口,他们用坚船利炮洞开了中华帝国闭锁已久的国门。而在此后不久,西方人挟着画板、携着刚刚发明出来的笨重的照相机,随着炮舰源源不断地涌进中国,把目光、镜头无数次地聚焦于这块对于他们而言神秘、新奇、美丽、富饶的土地。

摄影术约于1844年被西方人带到中国,并留下了一批有关中国的最早的照相资料。此后,涌入中国的西方军人、记者、传教士、商人、旅行家、探险家、外交官、科学家等,一步一步地深入到中国的每一个角落,用照片或图画记录着中国社会发生的巨大变化。也正是从此时开始,有关中国历史的记载,除了传统的文献档案资料的记述与绘画的描绘外,许多重大历史事件,都越来越多地被来到中国的西方摄影家们用相机凝结为永恒的"瞬间"。中国在西方人心目中的形象,也发生着天翻地覆的变迁:其中虽然仍不乏西方世界对中国辉煌灿烂的传统文化的敬畏,对中国风格独具的古代建筑的瞻仰,对中国恬淡淳朴的民风世俗的勾画,以及对中国雄伟壮丽的山川风景的惊羡;但是西方人用画笔与镜头记录下来的,更多的是西方世界对中华帝国国门的叩击以及这一古老帝国威严的坍圮,是踏海而来的西方世界的坚船利炮在神州土地上的耀武扬威,是中国朝廷的腐败、官场的昏暗、军队的怯懦与民众的愚昧,是西方列强在中国的攘权夺利,是进入民国时期的军阀混战与民不聊生……西人画笔与镜头聚焦的这段风云激荡的中国近代史,展示的近世中国无数个永恒的"瞬间",时间跨度久远,涉及中国社会方方面面,深刻而广泛,给中国乃至世人,留下了丰富多彩的内容。

同时，由于直观生动地记录了那个时代中国的历史风貌，这些"瞬间"成为我们今天历史研究的重要史料，同时也形成了西人对中国近世历史形象而真实的写照。

于是，历史给我们留下了一长串的名字：亚历山大（马戛尔尼使团随团画家）、阿洛姆（英国建筑师、画家）、于勒·埃及尔（法国海关总检察长，1844年来华）、李阁朗（早期来华摄影师）、比托（英国摄影师，第二次鸦片战争期间来华）、汤姆逊（早期来华摄影师）、奥尔末（早期来华摄影师）、南怀谦（来华传教士）、斯坦因（早期来华探险家，活动于中国西北地区）、沙畹（早期来华探险家）、赫定（早期来华探险家）、查尔德（1870—1880年在华）、马达汉（俄国早期来华探险家）、礼荷莲（女传教士，18世纪末活动于福建）、那爱德（早期来华传教士，《消失的天府》作者）、方苏雅（法国领事）、海斯（德国人，《山东》作者）、亨利王子（法国人，《从东京到印度》作者）、威尔逊（美国植物学家）、杰克逊（美国人，1895年来华活动）、小川一真（日本人）、佩奈尔（1900—1910年在华，收集大量中国摄影照片）、派尔森（法军上校）、山本讚七郎（日本人）、柏石曼（德国建筑师）、喜仁龙（瑞典人）、斯威尔（1906—1907年来华探险）、克拉克（1908—1909年来华考察，活动于陕甘地区）、莫里循（《泰晤士报》记者，清末民初长期活动于中国）、海达（20世纪30年代来华）、甘博（美国传教士，1920年前后来华）、洛克（美国探险家）、彭德尔顿（1931—1932年来华考察）、皮肯斯（美国传教士，1934—1936年拍摄北京等地清真寺）、饭山达雄（日本人，1936年来华）等，以及如《伦敦新闻画报》（1842—1940）、法国《巴黎小画报》《小巴黎人报》、美国《生活》杂志等报刊的记者等。可以说，从1840年至1949年的百余年间，在中国历史上的近代史时期，发生了无数次重大历史事件，在这些历史事件中，都有西方人的现场目击和摄影报道。这些报道及由之形成的影像资料，时间跨度从1793年至1949年，逾150年之久，范围则涉及中国社会之方方面面，凡军国大事、山川风光、人物肖像、庙谟民风、建筑物产、贩夫走卒、交通店肆，等等，无所不有，真实形象地记录和反映着当时中国的生产方式、生活方式、教育文化、宗教信仰等领域的情形，直观地展示着中国近世社会的变化轨迹、西人心中的中国形象的变化发展，内容广泛而深刻。

三

永恒的"瞬间"，连缀成可见的历史。

尤为可贵的是，近世以来西方人士用"第三只眼"展现的中国社会，形象、具体、丰富多彩。来到中国的西方人，身份不同、兴趣不同、聚焦点不同。他们或关注中国的山川俊美，物产丰饶；或关注中国的文化悠久，社会变迁；或关注中国的风俗民情，名胜建筑；或关注中国的军事政治，经济生活；或关注中国的政坛乱局，国民疾苦。他们用画板或镜头凝结的一个个近世中国的历史瞬间，具体而微且又全面广泛地连缀成了一部鲜活的中国近代历史。其中不少图像所反映出来的历史内容，甚至为官书档案，乃至方志文史所不载或载而未详。简单地举一个例子：美国霍普金斯大学地质学教授罗伯特·拉里莫尔·彭德尔顿（Robert Larimore Pendleton）早年长期活动于中国、印度、菲律宾和暹罗。1931年6月前后，彭德尔顿率探险队深入华北绥远地区考察土壤，恰遇1928年由时任绥远省政府主席李培基倡议兴建的萨拉齐民生渠接近竣工。彭德尔顿用手中的相机，拍下了数十幅照片，完整地记录了该渠在竣工前的修建、渠道、土方、堤坝、民工，以及竣工通水时的龙口、水闸、放水、观众、庆典等各方面的细节图像。最令人震撼的是，当年的民工们，居然是全身上下一丝不挂，裸着躯体，担土筑堤，开挖河渠。时至今日，当笔者试图查阅有关萨拉奇民生渠的历史资料时，却发现彭氏当年现场所拍摄的这些历史图像资料，尚未被人提及或加以运用，而在文献资料中，同样也不会有这种细节的记载与描述。这或许能够直接说明影像资料所具有的独特的明史、证史和补史的学术功能。

今天，当人类社会已经踏进一个新的世纪，回首百年之前的中国，其所经历的苦难与屈辱、抗争与梦想，都被近一个世纪的岁月洗礼得恬淡、安详。我们也能以一种平和的心情，来翻检百年前西方人士为我们留下的无数的近世中国影像，来审视这段用无数个被镜头与画幅凝为永恒的"瞬间"连缀而成的可见的历史，来认识、研究和反思中国近代社会的动荡、变迁与发展，同时也来感受西方人士当年对中国的观察、探寻与研究，来认识西方人士为我们留下的这笔丰富历史遗产所独具的学术文化价值。当然，摄影术被西方人士携入中国之后，很快被中国社会所接受。中国人也很快掌握了这门新兴的观察世界的技术，同样也涌现出无数的摄影家，拍摄出了无数照片，为我们留下了珍贵的历史影像资料。只是，本文考察的主体侧重于近世以来西方人士对中国的形象观察与表现，所以，同时代的中国摄影家的贡献，只能留待另文再作讨论了。

近代西方人士拍摄流传下来的有关中国的影像资料，存在形式多样，收藏分布广泛，存世数量庞大。近若干年来，随着大量的有关中国题材的历史图像不断面世，"影像史料"和"影像史学"也逐渐成为历史学界热门话题之一，越来越受到学术界的关注，许多学术专著或普及性读物都利用了大量的影像史料，图文并茂，受到读者的欢迎；专题性图片集的出版也日益丰富，对历史知识的传播和历史学术研究都起到了积极的推动作用。与此同时，国际史学界中对"影像史学"的探讨与推动方兴未艾，影像与史学研究的关系越来越受到关注与重视。历史影像本身不仅被视为历史学研究重要的新的史料来源，而且影像信息之表达形式甚至影响到历史学的表达方式、人们认识与观念的传播方式。王国维尝言，新学问的出现大都是由于新材料的推动，材料可以帮助方法，而材料的不同又可以使做学问的结果与成绩不同。拟之于影像，则历史图像资料之作为一种新的材料，其形象、具体、生动的历史图像本身所蕴含的丰富的历史信息，同样也必将推动历史学乃至其他学科的新学问的诞生与发展。

近些年随着中国综合国力的增强和国际地位的提升，有关中国题材的各种历史图像或老照片受到全球读者的关注，埋没数十年乃至百年之久的中国历史图像、老照片等，从西方的图书馆、博物馆，乃至私人收藏家的尘封中陆续得以重见天日，而且有层出不穷之势。这为我们提供了绝佳的历史契机，使我们有机会更系统全面地搜集近世以来西方世界有关中国的绘画作品与摄影作品，在彰显国家进步与文化繁荣的同时，有目的、有意识地积累、保存、保护这些承载着我们民族文化历史丰富信息的珍贵资料，进而更深刻、全面和形象地认识、理解风云激荡的中国近代历史。所以，我们相信，有计划、有目的地搜集、整理和出版中国近世影像史料，尤其是近世以来西方人士拍摄描绘的有关中国的影像资料（包括绘画、照片、纪录电影），利用现代高度发达的科学技术，以适当的方式提供给大众及专业研究者使用参考，必将会给中国近代史研究带来许多新鲜的史料，拓展新的学术研究领域。这项工作不仅体现了对中国古代以图载史、图书并重传统的继承与弘扬，而且顺应人类文化发展潮流，从而将史学研究带入"图像时代"，对中国"影像史学"的建立与发展起到积极作用，对促进国家文化建设也具有重要的现实意义。

古人云："以铜为镜，可以正衣冠；以古为镜，可以知兴替。"事实上，西人画笔与镜头中的近世中国影像，既是中国近世历史的写照，某种程度上也反映着西方对中国的认识。不论是其影像所反映的中国近世历史，还是西人对中国近世的认识本身，都是值得我们去揭示、认识、理解和反思的课题。因此，我们经过搜集、整理、编辑、出版了这套《西方的中国影像》（1793—1949），意在通过被西方人当年用"第三只眼"凝固的中国近世的一个个历史"瞬间"，形象地展示中国近世社会的变化轨迹，以及西人心中的中国形象的变化发展。

Seeing China in Modern Times Through the Third Eye

Bian Xiuyue

To see China in modern times through the third eye is a vivid and colorful experience.

Foreign people in modern times got to know China mostly from William Alexander, a painter accompanying the diplomatic mission led by was British envoy Macartney in 1793. It is no doubt that China had already risen to fame among Europe before that and this fever had lasted for a long while. From the first time China was heard to the Age of Enlightenment, the western world always regarded China, an ancient oriental empire, as a model in wealth and civilization. A series of admiration and longing was triggered after that. Though Macartney's visit to China could not make this big empire to open its door, thus to fulfill his mission to do business with China, his accompanying painter William Alexander put the information he collected during the journey like the scenery along the road, temples and architecture, local customs, officials and servants, generals and soldiers, into paintings. Not until 1843 did this situation experience some changes after Fisher Company from London, British published *China:The Scenery, Architecture, and Social Habits of That Ancient Empire*, a large series of picture album with text illustrations. This album is drawn by Thomas Allom, a British architect and landscapist and annotated by a historian called George Wright. This was an epitomized album about China related themes in the Europe and provided abundant historical information of Chinese social life to the western world before the photography became mature. And just when this album was unveiled to the public, the British built a harbor crowned by the name of Queen Victoria on Hong Kong Island. They forced the door of China open by their weapons. Shortly after this, westerners poured into China by gunships with drawing boards in arms and heavy cameras in hands, which were just invented out. Numerous times were the spotlights and lens focused on this mysterious, novel, beautiful and affluent oriental land.

Several years after photography was invented, it was brought to China by the westerners in 1844 and, hence, the earliest image data of China was left. Later on, military forces, journalists, preachers, merchants, travelers, explorers, diplomats and scientists from the western world swarmed into China. They slid into every corner of China gradually and recorded the huge change taking place in China through photos and paintings. And just from the very time, records of Chinese history especially big events, apart from archives and paintings, more and more turned into snapshots under the lens of the western photographers. Meanwhile, image of China in the eyes of the westerners experienced a great change. Though there still existed reverence towards Chinese traditional culture, worship to Chinese uniquely styled ancient buildings, illustrations of unsophisticated local customs as well as admiration of the magnificent mountains and rivers in China, what the westerners' brushes and lens focused more were the hard knock on China's door by the western world and the collapse of the dignity of an ancient empire. More attention were paid to the strong muscles of gunpowder showed by the western world on China's land, to the corruption of the government and officialdom, to the cowardliness of military troops and ignorance of the common people. They cared much more about how the outcomers interfered with Chinese's politics and expanded their interests and how life fell into a chaotic state when it came to the Republican period, during which various warlords were in a tangled warfare. The unquiet China's modern history recorded by brushes and lens of the westerners caught numerous everlasting moments of China. They almost cover every aspect of the society, the profoundness and wideness of which offer rich and colorful topics to see by people around the world. They documented Chinese history of that time directly and vividly which become important materials for today's historical research.

During the ten decades of years from 1840 to 1949, the modern times of Chinese history witnessed countless big events taking place, which were all witnessed on site or photographed by the westerners. Reports and graphic materials generated thereafter cover a time span of 150 years from 1793 to 1949. They include comprehensive aspects of the Chinese society from national affairs, scenic spots, portraits, temples and local customs to architecture, peddlers, transportation and so on. The production, lifestyle, education, religions and other fields at that time were authentically recorded to show the traces of change of China in modern times, as well as the change of China's image in the eyes of the westerners.

The ancient wisdom says that using a bronze mirror, we can exam how we dress; studying history, we can understand why there were rises and falls of powers. In fact, China's images through the brushes and lens of the westerners are not only the real portrayal of Chinese modern history, but also the westerners' recognition of China. Yet no matter of what, it is a theme that deserves us to uncover, to know about , to understand and to rethink. That is why we collect, edit and publish China's Images in Modern Times, aiming to draw the traces of change in China in modern times and the change of China's images in the heart of the westerners through each historical moment captured by the third eye.

凡例

一、本书选录自1793年英国特使马戛尔尼使华到1949年以前约一个半世纪西方来华的外交官、军人、传教士、探险家、记者、商人等有关中国的绘画或照片等,以及在此时期内西方报刊或在中国境内出版的西文报刊发表的有关中国的图片资料。

二、本书所谓的"西方",不仅仅是指地理概念上的西方,更取社会与文化发展意义上的西方,故包含有近代较早接受西方文化、较早进入近代化社会阶段的国家,如日本等。

三、本书以绘画者、摄影者、图片收藏者或近代有关中国影像书籍的编辑者为单元分卷;西方报刊或在中国境内出版的西文报刊上的图片资料,则以报刊名称为单元分卷。同一作者(单元)作品数量较多者,可单独成卷或分多卷;同一作者(单元)作品数量较少,不足以独立成卷者,则由多个作者(单元)并作一卷。

四、本书每单元首列作者简介或报刊简介。图片以作品产生年代或发表年代先后排序;无精确时间标识者,则以时间段排序;拍摄时间、地点不明的,置于同一作者(单元)卷末。

五、每幅图片作简单说明,主要介绍图片记录的事件、人物、地点、时间等内容,不作牵强附会解释,不作主观随意评价。拍摄时间、地点不明的,不作标注。

六、书中所涉地名纷繁琐碎,中、外文地名通译难度较大,个别音译地名括附外文原名。图片产生时行政区划与现代行政区划不同的,本书原则上依据图片的原始信息,沿用当时的行政区划。而对历史上变动频繁的行政区划,难以考证者,间以现代行政区划为准。

Notes

1. This book excerpts historical image data which records the situation of the English special envoy Macartney's coming to China in 1793 and the Chinese paintings and photos of the ambassadors, soldiers, preachers, explorers, journalists, merchants and so on, who came to China for one and a half centuries before 1949. It also includes pictures published by the foreign press or domestic newspapers or magazines in western languages during those periods.

2. The "western" we refer in this book does not only mean the geographical one, but one from the point of social and cultural aspects as well. That`s why countries like Japan, which assimilated western culture and entered into modern social stage in the earlier times, is included in the book.

3. This book is categorized by painters, photographers, collectors and the editors for books on China's images in modern times individually. For pictures on the foreign press or domestic newspapers or magazines in western languages, they are sorted out according to specific newspapers or magazines. The author or unit that covers too many works will be separated into an independent book or books. On the contrary, if the works of the author or unit are not abundant enough to generate an independent book, works of these will be put together in one.

4. Introductions of the authors or the press will be listed firstly in every unit of the book. Pictures are sorted out in a chronological order of their generation time or published time. Works with no definite time will be sequenced according to the time bucket. Photos without definite time and place are placed at the end of the unit.

5. Every picture is followed by a brief introduction explaining the incident, persons, location, time included in the picture. There is neither far-fetched interpretation nor subjective commentation. No note will be added to photos without definite time and place.

6. Since the names of places mentioned in the book are too complex and translation of domestic and foreign places are too difficult, transliteration is adopted for some special cases, its original foreign names included. The administrative division when the birth of those photos is different from what is now in the modern times. This book follows the original information in principle and adopts the administrative division. For names which frequently changed and are hard to verified, modern way of administrative division is used instead.

目录

亚瑟·威廉·佩奈尔
Arthur William Purnell

亚瑟·威廉·佩奈尔
Arthur William Purnell

　　亚瑟·威廉·佩奈尔（Arthur William Purnell，1878—1964年），生于澳大利亚维多利亚州，曾在戈登学院学习建筑，在季隆艺术学校学习绘画。1895年，进入其父亲的建筑公司作制图员。1899年，到非洲、欧洲、美国及新西兰学习建筑。1900来到中国。1903年，被任命为香港公共工程部职员，旋入英国丹备建筑公司，被派到广州，主管丹备洋行沙面分行。1904年，他与帕捷合伙开办了"治平洋行"（Purnell & Paget，后称"伯捷洋行"），专门承接建筑设计、土木和测绘工程。在广州设计建造了大清邮政局、岭南学堂的马丁堂、沙面的英人俱乐部、花旗银行新楼、万国宝通银行、瑞记洋行、礼和洋行、东亚贸易公司等建筑，其中，瑞记洋行和马丁堂被称为中国近代最早的钢筋混凝土结构建筑。佩奈尔在1911年前后离开中国广州回到澳洲。

　　Arthur William Purnell(1978—1964) was born in the State of Victoria in Australia. He used to learn architecture in Gorden College and painting in Geelong Art School. In 1895, he went into his father's company to be a cartographer and flew to Africa, Europe, America and New Zealand to learn architecture. He came to China in 1900 and became an employee of Hong Kong Public Works Department in 1903. He was then transferred to British Danbay Architecture Company and assigned to Guangzhou in charge of the branch of Danbay Foreign Firm on Shamian Island. In 1904, he and his partner Paget opened up Zhiping Foreign Firm(Purnell & Paget Foreign Firm, also called Bojie Foreign Firm later on), which especially undertook architecture design, construction and mapping. It built the post office of the Qing Dynasty, Martin Hall of Canton Christian College, British club on Shamian Island, the new building of Citibank, the Peoples State Bank, Ruiji Foreign Firm, Lihe Foreign Firm and East-Asia Trade Company. Among them, Ruiji Foreign Firm and Martin Hall are honored as the earliest buildings of reinforced concrete structure. Purnell came back to Australia from Guangzhou around 1911.

山脚下的城市建筑	>	Urban architecture at the foot of the mountain
香港	–	Hongkong
1906年 — 1908年	–	1906 —1908

山顶花园与休息的人们 > Garden at the mountaintop and the relaxed people

香港 - Hongkong

1906年—1908年 - 1906—1908

新一任总督到达，港口码头举行仪式迎接　　>　　A new governor is arriving and a welcome ceremony is held at the port.

香港　　—　　Hongkong

1906年 — 1908年　　—　　1906 — 1908

梅特卡夫中将在干船坞的舷梯上 > Lieutenant general Metika on the accommodation ladder of the dry dock

香港 — Hongkong

1906年—1910年 — 1906—1910

台风过后，港口倾翻的大型蒸汽轮船 > Large steamers overturned and damaged after typhoon

香港 — Hongkong

1906年 — 1906

西方的中国影像

台风过后，民众捡拾有用的物品　>　Citizens picking up useful goods after typhoon

香港　—　Hongkong

1906年　—　1906

台风过后，海滨倒塌的房屋，而后面的红砖建筑依然完好　>　Collapsed houses and intact red-bricked architecture after typhoon

香港　—　Hongkong

1906年　—　1906

城市的建筑 > Urban architecture

香港 — Hongkong

1907年 — 1907

台风过后，停在港口的轮船　>　Ships halting at the port after typhoon

香港　—　Hongkong

1907年　—　1907

停在码头的广东蒸汽轮　>　A Guangdong steamer anchoring at the wharf

香港　—　Hongkong

1907年　—　1907

海港与海面上的船只	>	The harbor and ships in the sea
香港	-	Hongkong
1907年	-	1907

海港与海面上的船只 > The harbor and ships in the sea

香港 — Hongkong

1907年 — 1907

英国国王爱德华七世的生日，英国军人在沙面岛举行庆祝活动　>　Birthday of Edward VII, King of England, a celebration is held on Shamian Island by English soldiers.

广东　—　Guangdong

1901年 — 1910年　—　1901 — 1910

天主教堂 > A Catholic Church

广东 – Guangdong

1905年 – 1905

沙面帝国海关大楼建设棚　　>　A construction site of the Imperial Customs House on Shamian Island

广东　　—　Guangdong

1906年　　—　1906

海珠区的水泥厂 > A cement plant in Haizhu District

广东 — Guangdong

1907年 — 1907

军火库爆炸摧毁的城墙　>　City walls damaged by the explosion of the arsenal

广东　　—　Guangdong

1907年　—　1907

军火库爆炸后的情景 > Sight after the explosion of the arsenal

广东 — Guangdong

1907年 — 1907

台风之前的沙面法国领事馆花园 > The garden of the French Consulate on Shamian Island before typhoon

广东 — Guangdong

1908年 — 1908

台风过后,英租界内的运河沿岸房顶被吹落、树木被吹倒的情形

广东

1908 年

Roofs blown off and trees swept down along the canal governed in the English Concession after typhoon

Guangdong

1908

台风过后,英租界江边的法国轮船 > After typhoon, a French ship at the riverside in the English Concession

广东 — Guangdong

1908年 — 1908

台风过后，英租界内建筑轻微受损，有些树木被吹倒 > The small damage of the architecture and falling trees in the English Concession after typhoon

广东 — Guangdong

1908年 — 1908

大火前的花船太沙燕（音，Tai Sha Yan）号 > Tai Sha Yan, a decorated ship before the fire

广东 — Guangdong

1909年 — 1909

史密斯·斯坦顿在沙面举行的婚礼 > Smith Stanton holding his wedding on Shamian Island

广东 - Guangdong

1909年 - 1909

在广东舞蹈俱乐部的宴会厅，外国人举行庆祝华盛顿诞辰集会 > At the banquet hall of the Guangdong Dance Club, foreigners are holding a gathering to celebrate the birthday of George Washington.

广东 — Guangdong

1909年 — 1909

一个被破坏的建筑物，可能在广州 > A damaged building, maybe in Guangzhou

1906年—1910年 1906—1910

广东皇家邮政局 > Guangdong Royal Mail

广东 — Guangdong

1906年—1910年 — 1906—1910

街头的剧院 > A theatre in a street

广东 — Guangdong

1906年—1910年 — 1906—1910

在晴朗的天气观看城内的民房屋顶 > Roofs of urban civilian houses seen in a sunny day

广东 — Guangdong

1906年—1910年 — 1906—1910

城内东面街区景象 > Sight of the eastern part of the city

广东 — Guangdong

1906年—1910年 — 1906—1910

火灾之后的残垣断壁 > Ruins after the fire

广东 — Guangdong

1906年—1910年 — 1906—1910

被大火烧得只剩下残壁的建物 > Rubbles left by the fire

广东 — Guangdong

1906年—1910年 — 1906—1910

火灾之后的情形 > Situation after the fire

广东 — Guangdong

1906年—1910年 — 1906—1910

火灾之后的情形 > Situation after the fire

广东 — Guangdong

火灾之后，展开善后重建 > Reconstruction after the fire

广东 – Guangdong

1906年 — 1910年 – 1906—1910

中心城区依然浓烟滚滚 > Smoke lingering over the city centre

广东 — Guangdong

1906年—1910年 — 1906—1910

依水而建的房子   >   A house built along the water

广东   —   Guangdong

1906年—1910年   —   1906—1910

从城墙上俯瞰乡间小道 > A country road overseen from the city wall

广东 — Guangdong

1906年—1910年 — 1906—1910

火灾之后的英国桥（British Bridge）	>	The British Bridge after the fire
广东	-	Guangdong
1906年—1910年	-	1906—1910

倒塌的房子	>	Collapsed houses
广东	–	Guangdong
1906年—1910年	–	1906—1910

水岸边上的传统民居 > Traditional dwellings at the riverside

广东 — Guangdong

1906年—1910年 — 1906—1910

精心装饰的古建筑屋顶，多为花岗岩和瓷砖 > Elaborately decorated roof of an old architecture, which is ornamented by granites and tiles

广东 — Guangdong

1906年—1910年 — 1906—1910

乡间的临水建筑与河水中的水牛 > Buildings constructed along the water in the countryside and buffalos in the lake

广东 — Guangdong

1906年—1910年 — 1906—1910

运河	>	The canal
广东	–	Guangdong
1906年—1910年	–	1906—1910

运河两岸景观 > Views on both sides of the canal

广东 — Guangdong

1906年—1910年 — 1906—1910

在河中下网捕鱼	>	Casting nets in the river
广东	-	Guangdong
1906年—1910年	-	1906—1910

稻田的灌溉渠道	>	Irrigation channels in paddy fields
广东	-	Guangdong
1906年—1910年	-	1906—1910

城郊附近农村的稻田 > Rice fields in the countryside

广东 - Guangdong

1906年—1910年 - 1906—1910

郊区农村传统的民房，屋前立着旗杆的房子是家族祠堂

广东

1906年—1910年

Traditional countryside residence in suburban area, the house with flagpoles in the front is a family ancestral hall.

Guangdong

1906—1910

乡间一景 > A view of the countryside

广东 - Guangdong

1906年—1910年 - 1906—1910

| 狭窄的石板街道和两边的商号 | > | A narrow road covered by slate and shops on both sides |

广东 — Guangdong

1906年—1910年 — 1906—1910

6 层的红砖建筑——典当行，后面有很多竹竿的地方是染坊

> A six-story red brick building—a pawnshop, and a dyehouse among many bamboos in the behind

广东 — Guangdong

1906年—1910年 — 1906—1910

> 乡村的男孩 Boys in the country

| 掏耳朵 | > | Ear cleaning service |

| 广东 | – | Guangdong |

| 1906年—1910年 | – | 1906—1910 |

鸦片吸食者们 > Opium-smoking men

广东 — Guangdong

1906年 — 1910年 — 1906—1910

斗鸡比赛时用的鸡笼 > Coops used during the rooster fighting game

广东 — Guangdong

1906年—1910年 — 1906—1910

街头卖艺者与围观的人群 > A street performer and the crowd

广东 - Guangdong

1906年 — 1910年 - 1906—1910

观看放风筝的人群 > People watching kites flying

广东 — Guangdong

1906年—1910年 — 1906—1910

八角塔（胡椒罐式）和坚固的城墙 > The eight-angle tower (pepper pot like) and fortified city walls

广东 — Guangdong

1906年—1910年 — 1906—1910

海关观察塔下的江面与船只 > The river and boats at the foot of the customs supervision tower

广东 — Guangdong

1906年—1910年 — 1906—1910

中国南方浸信会建筑工地	>	A Baptist construction site in southern China
广东	–	Guangdong
1906年 — 1910年	–	1906—1910

城郊的花岗岩牌坊 > A granite memorial archway in the countryside

广东 — Guangdong

1906年—1910年 — 1906—1910

城郊的花岗岩牌坊 > A granite memorial archway in the countryside

广东 — Guangdong

1906年—1910年 — 1906—1910

镇海楼及楼侧的老式火炮（原注：这些大炮是无害的） > Zhenhai Building and old cannons near the side of the bulding(These cannons are harmless.)

广东 — Guangdong

1906年—1910年 — 1906—1910

七层宝塔　　>　A seven-storey pagoda

广东　　－　Guangdong

1906年—1910年　－　1906—1910

一座高大的佛塔 > A grand pagoda

广东 — Guangdong

1906年—1910年 — 1906—1910

五仙观，位于今惠福西路，建于明洪武七年（1337年），是祭祀五仙的谷神庙 > Five Fairies Temple, located in Huifu West Road and built in the seventh year of the Hongwu period of the Ming Dynasty(1337). It is a grain harvest God temple in the worship of five fairies.

广东 — Guangdong

1906年—1910年 — 1906—1910

华林寺正殿佛像。华林寺位于今广州市荔湾区下九路西来正街，始建於梁武帝普通八年（527年），迄今已有1400多年的历史

广东

1906年—1910年

Buddha statues in the main hall of Hualin Temple. Hualin Temple lies in Xilaizheng Street, Shangxiajiu Road, Liwan District. Guangzhou, it was built in the eighth year of the Putong period under the reign of Emperor Wu of the Liang Dynasty. It has a history (527) of over 1400 years.

Guangdong

1906—1910

华林寺五百罗汉堂	>	Five-hundred Arhats Hall of Hualin Temple
广东	—	Guangdong
1906年—1910年	—	1906—1910

华林寺东殿 > The east hall of Hualin Temple

广东 — Guangdong

1906年—1910年 — 1906—1910

华林寺五百罗汉堂的罗汉塑像	>	Arhat statues in the Five-hundred Arhats Hall of Hualin Temple
广东	—	Guangdong
1906年—1910年	—	1906—1910

六榕寺花塔。六榕寺历史悠久,始建于梁大同三年(537年),以六榕花塔为特色标志,曾是禅宗道场,与海幢寺、光孝寺、华林寺、大佛寺并称为广东佛教"五大丛林"

广东

1906年 — 1910年

> The Flower Tower of Six Banyan Temple. The temple has a long history dating back to the third year of the Datong period of the Liang Dynasty(527) . It is symbolized by the six banyan flowers and was once the bodhimanda of Zen. Together with Haizhuang Temple, Guangxiao Temple, Huanglin Temple and Dafo Temple, it is placed as one of the Five Buddhist Temples in Guangdong.

- Guangdong

- 1906—1910

珠江支河上的场景 > The scene of a branch of the Pearl River

广东 — Guangdong

1906年—1910年 — 1906—1910

粤汉铁路上的一个小站	>	A small station of the Yue-Han railway
广东	—	Guangdong
1906年 — 1910年	—	1906 — 1910

珠江边正在新建湖南会馆 > Hunan Guild Hall built alongside the Pearl River

广东 — Guangdong

1906年—1910年 — 1906—1910

修复受损的堤岸 > Repairing the damaged bank

广东 — Guangdong

1906年—1910年 — 1906—1910

繁忙的珠江水运　>　Busy water carriage in the Pearl River

广东　—　Guangdong

1906年—1910年　—　1906—1910

珠江上的蒸汽游轮和帆船	>	Steamers and sailing ships in the Pearl River
广东	—	Guangdong
1906年—1910年	—	1906—1910

珠江上的帆船 > Sailing boats in the Pearl River

广东 – Guangdong

1906年—1910年 – 1906—1910

繁忙的珠江航道，对岸是广州剧院 > Busy channels of the Pearl River and the Guangzhou Theatre on the other side of the bank

广东 — Guangdong

1906年—1910年 — 1906—1910

珠江上的繁忙水运 > Busy water carriage in the Pearl River

广东 — Guangdong

1906年 — 1910年 — 1906—1910

江面停锚的警船和蒸汽游轮 > Police ships and steamers moored in the river

广东 — Guangdong

1906年—1910年 — 1906—1910

繁忙的航道与江面上的船只 > Busy channels and boats in the river

广东 — Guangdong

1906年—1910年 — 1906—1910

蒸汽船和小舢板停泊在拥挤的码头，古老与现代，东方与西方的明显对比

广东

1906年—1910年

> Steamers and small sampans crowding into the harbor, contrasts between the old and the modern, the East and the West

– Guangdong

– 1906—1910

疏浚珠江河道，以及江面上桅杆林立的船只

广东

1906年—1910年

Dredging the channels of the Pearl River and many boats with masts in the river

Guangdong

1906—1910

繁忙的珠江航道 > Busy channels of the Pearl River

广东 — Guangdong

1906年—1910年 — 1906—1910

珠江两岸拥挤的住房和江中往返的舢板 > Crowded residence at both sides of the Pearl River and sampans going back and forth in the river

广东 — Guangdong

1906年—1910年 — 1906—1910

江面上的蒸汽游轮和小舢板 > Steamers and small sampans in the river

广东 — Guangdong

1906年—1910年 — 1906—1910

| 珠江江面上的蒸汽游轮和小舢板 | > | Steamers and small sampans in the Pearl River |

广东 — Guangdong

1906年—1910年 — 1906—1910

| 珠江上的大型渡船 | > | A large ferryboat in the Pearl River |

广东 — Guangdong

1906年—1910年 — 1906—1910

珠江边停泊的舢板与岸上的建筑 > Sampans stopped at the riverside and buildings on the bank

广东 — Guangdong

1906年—1910年 — 1906—1910

珠江上的舢板	>	Sampans in the Pearl River
广东	–	Guangdong
1906年—1910年	–	1906—1910

珠江两岸的繁忙景象 > Hustle and bustle on both sides of the Pearl River

广东 — Guangdong

1906年—1910年 — 1906—1910

珠江上的龙舟比赛 > Dragon boat races in the Pearl River

广东 — Guangdong

1906年—1910年 — 1906—1910

珠江上正在举行龙舟赛 > Dragon boat races in the Pearl River

广东 — Guangdong

1906年—1910年 — 1906—1910

三艘船并列负载货物 > Three boats abreast loading cargo

广东 — Guangdong

1906年—1910年 — 1906—1910

旧时的船楼，其中留下了许多风流韵事　>　Houses on deck, many romances happening there

广东　　　　　　　　　　　　　　　　　-　Guangdong

1906年 — 1910年　　　　　　　　　　　-　1906—1910

从高处看珠江三角洲全景 > Panorama of the Pearl River Delta overseen from high

广东 — Guangdong

1906年—1910年 — 1906—1910

水田里劳作的农民 > Farmers working in the paddy fields

广东 — Guangdong

1906年—1910年 — 1906—1910

江边的鸭群，江面上的桅船 > Ducks along the river and brigs in the river

广东 - Guangdong

1906年—1910年 - 1906—1910

珠江上的舢板与船民们	>	Sampans and boat people of the Pearl River
广东	–	Guangdong
1906年 — 1910年	–	1906—1910

穷人的"拖鞋船"挤在河边 > "Slipper-like" boats crowding at the riverside

广东 — Guangdong

1906年—1910年 — 1906—1910

渡船上不习惯面对镜头的中国人　>　Chinese people on a ferryboat who are not accustomed to camera lens

广东　—　Guangdong

1906年 — 1910年　—　1906—1910

渡船上不习惯面对镜头的中国人　>　Chinese people on a ferryboat who are not accustomed to camera lens

广东　—　Guangdong

1906年 — 1910年　—　1906—1910

拥挤在岸边的小船和在船上贩卖的蔬菜 > Boats crowding near the bank and vegetables sold on boats

广东 — Guangdong

1906年—1910年 — 1906—1910

江面上的澳大利亚海军的蒸汽船 > An Australian navy steamer in the river

广东 — Guangdong

1906年 — 1910年 — 1906—1910

停在码头的法国游轮，7月14日将在这举行晚会 — A French cruise stopped at the wharf, an evening party to be held in July 14th

广东 — Guangdong

1906年—1910年 — 1906—1910

珠江上的轮船，可以一次承载 200 名乘客。远处是法国游轮 > A Ship in the Pearl River, with a loading capacity of 200 passengers. The distance is a French cruise.

广东 — Guangdong

1906 年 — 1910 年 — 1906—1910

内政部的官方盐船 > An official salt carrier of the Ministry of the Interior

广东 — Guangdong

1906 年 — 1910 年 — 1906—1910

西江江面与江上的兵轮 > The surface of the West River and military ships

广东 — Guangdong

1906年—1910年 — 1906—1910

西江江面与岸边建筑 > The surface of the West River and buildings on the bank

广东 — Guangdong

1906年—1910年 — 1906—1910

西江 > The West River

广东 — Guangdong

1906年—1910年 — 1906—1910

西江风光 > Views of the West River

广东 – Guangdong

1906年—1910年 – 1906—1910

还在修建中的天字号（音，Tye Chung Hau）轮船码头泊位

广东

1906年—1910年

The berth of the Tye Chung Hau Wharf in construction

Guangdong

1906—1910

即将建成的天字号码头（音，Tye Chung Hau） > The Tye Chung Hau Wharf to be completed

广东 — Guangdong

1906年 — 1910年 — 1906—1910

即将建成的天字号码头（音，Tye Chung Hau） > The Tye Chung Hau Wharf to be completed

广东 — Guangdong

1906 — 1910

已经建成的天字号码头（音，Tye Chung Hau） > The completed Tye Chung Hau Wharf

广东 — Guangdong

1906年—1910年 — 1906—1910

码头完成修缮后，第一个到达的"九龙"号蒸汽轮船 > The first Kowloon steamer arriveing at the wharf after it was renovated

广东 — Guangdong

1906年—1910年 — 1906—1910

在码头停泊的海洋轮船"Lydia"号 > The Lydia, a marine ship, moored at the wharf

广东 — Guangdong

1906年—1910年 — 1906—1910

广东电力供应建设，架设锅炉，右一是亚瑟·佩奈尔 > Construction of Guangdong electric power supply, erection of the boiler, the first one from the right is Arthur Purnel.

广东 — Guangdong

1906年—1910年 — 1906—1910

天字号码头（音，Tye Chung Hau）的钢筋水泥混凝土柱的钢结构 > The steel structure of the Tye Chung Hau Wharf which is made of reinforced concrete cement

广东 — Guangdong

1906年—1910年 — 1906—1910

沙面即将完工建成的电灯站，以及停泊在附近江面的船只

广东

1906年 — 1910年

> The electric light station to be completed on Shamian Island and boats moored in the river nearby

— Guangdong

1906—1910

沙面即将完工建成的电灯站，以及停泊在附近江面的船只

广东

1906年—1910年

The electric light station to be completed on Shamian Island and boats moored in the river nearby

Guangdong

1906—1910

沙面法租界内的运河，舢板须向监管警察办公室支付费用方可进入

广东

1906年 — 1910年

The canal governed in the French Concession of Shamian Island. Sampans needed to pay money to the supervision police office

Guangdong

1906 — 1910

沙面河上的帆船 > Sailing ships in the river of Shamian Island

广东 — Guangdong

1906年—1910年 — 1906—1910

沙面江面上的外国兵轮与江边的小船 > A foreign military ship in the river of Shamian Island and boats near the riverside

广东 — Guangdong

1906年—1910年 — 1906—1910

沙面教会（圣公会）的 建筑和前面的外滩	>	Architecture of the church (Anglican Church) on Shamian Island and the bund in front of it
广东	–	Guangdong
1906年—1910年	–	1906—1910

| 沙面教会（圣公会）前的道路 | > | Roads ahead of the church (Anglican Church) on Shamian Island |

广东 — Guangdong

1906年—1910年 — 1906—1910

| 沙面教会（圣公会）向西的中央大道 | > | The central west-facing avenue of the church (Anglican Church) on Shamian Island |

广东 — Guangdong

1906年—1910年 — 1906—1910

沙面教会（圣公会）向西的中央大道　　>　The central west-facing avenue of the church (Anglican Church) on Shamian Island

广东　　—　Guangdong

1906年—1910年　　—　1906—1910

沙面教会（圣公会）向西的中央大道　　>　The central west-facing avenue of the church (Anglican Church) on Shamian Island

广东　　—　Guangdong

1906年—1910年　　—　1906—1910

沙面法国领事馆、帕斯奎特& Cie 公司 > The French Consulate and Pasquet & Cie Company on Shamian Island

广东 — Guangdong

1906年—1910年 — 1906—1910

沙面法国领事馆、帕斯奎特& Cie 公司 > The French Consulate and Pasquet & Cie Company on Shamian Island

沙面英国卡罗威兹公司 > British Calloways Company on Shamian Island

广东 - Guangdong

1906年—1910年 - 1906—1910

沙面英国卡罗威兹公司 > British Calloways Company on Shamian Island

沙面外滩公园和树木成荫的道路　　The garden in the bund of Shamian Island and the shady road

广东

1906——1910　　1906—1910

| 沙面外滩公园的树木和道路 | > | Trees and roads in the garden in the bund of Shamian Island |

广东 — Guangdong

1906年 — 1910年 — 1906—1910

| 沙面外滩的自行车练习道 | > | The track for bicycles in the bund of Shamian Island |

广东 — Guangdong

1906年—1910年 — 1906—1910

沙面外滩公园内的网球场和自行车练习道 > A tennis court in the garden and a track for bicycles

广东 — Guangdong

1906年—1910年 — 1906—1910

沙面沿林荫大道两旁的骑楼建筑　>　Arcades on both shady sides of Shamian Island

广东　—　Guangdong

1906年 — 1910年　—　1906—1910

一位时髦的女士	>	A stylish lady
广东	—	Guangdong
1906年—1910年	—	1906—1910

一个戴硬草帽的欧洲人站在乡村的一处水潭边	>	A European wearing a boater standing at the poolside in the countryside
广东	—	Guangdong
1906年—1910年	—	1906—1910

游览白云山 > Visiting Baiyun Mountain

广东 — Guangdong

1906年—1910年 — 1906—1910

在城外的一处凉亭里歇息的人们 > People resting in a pavilion out of town

广东 — Guangdong

1906年—1910年 — 1906—1910

军营庭院	>	The courtyard of the military camp
广东	–	Guangdong
1906年—1910年	–	1906—1910

漂浮在江上的陈尸所，上面还有一个焚化炉 > Morgues floating in the river with incinerators on them

广东 — Guangdong

1906年—1910年 — 1906—1910

装入陶罐中正准备埋葬的死者遗骨(俗称金罐) > Corpses in the clay pots (golden pot) ready to be buried

广东 — Guangdong

1906年—1910年 — 1906—1910

附近山坡上的墓区，在此墓地区域进行的黄金开采探测尚未开始	>	A cemetery area on a hill nearby, where gold mining and exploitation hadn't been carried out in this area yet
广东	–	Guangdong
1906年—1910年	–	1906—1910

山坡上的墓葬群，准备黄金开采探测的地域	>	Cemetery colonies on the hill, where gold mining and exploitation would be carried out
广东	–	Guangdong
1906年—1910年	–	1906—1910

赛南（音，Sainan）村口的河头上等待搭船的人们 > People waiting to take a boat at the head of the river in Sainan village

广东 — Guangdong

1906年—1910年 — 1906—1910

一艘兵轮 > A military ship

桑迪曼（音，Sandiman）公司有关中国和印度进口茶叶的广告 > Ads of Sandiman Company about tea imported from China and India

广东 — Guangdong

1906年—1910年 — 1906—1910

在"青岛"（音，Tsingtau）号上 > On the Tsingtau ship

1906年—1910年 — 1906—1910

编 委 会

主　　任　李学通

编委会委员　卞修跃　古为明　刘　萍　李学通　张会芳
　　　　　　　吴胜利　程朝云　徐　宏　鲍　宁　詹利萍

西方的中国影像

1 7 9 3 — 1 9 4 9

亚瑟·威廉·佩奈尔卷　二

主编　卞修跃　|　本卷主编　卞修跃

黄山书社

中国巨人詹五九照片 > The photo of the Chinese giant, Zhan Wujiu

J. R. Tanner 拍摄 — Shot by J.R.Tanner

1871年 — 1871

中国巨人和他的妻子、朋友的照片　>　The photo of the Chinese giant and his wife and friend

J. R. Tanner 拍摄　—　Shot by J.R.Tanner

1871年　—　1871

中国巨人　>　The Chinese giant

A. W. Burman 拍摄　—　Shot by A. W. Burman

1876年　—　1876

梧州西江沿岸的修道院花园 > The monastery garden on the bank of the Xi River in Wuzhou

广西 — Guangxi

1900年—1910年 — 1900—1910

梧州西江侯莱克瀑布（音，the Hou Lik Falls） > The Hou Lik Falls on the bank of the Xi River in Wuzhou

广西 — Guangxi

1900年—1910年 — 1900—1910

梧州侯莱克瀑布下 > Under the Hou Lik Falls in Wuzhou

广西 – Guangxi

1900年—1910年 – 1900—1910

梧州一些乡民们正在等待着进入侯莱克瀑布，想从泉眼为家人汲取圣水

广西

1900 年 — 1910 年

Some villagers are waiting for being letting into the source of the Hou Lik Falls to fetch the holy water for their families.

- Guangxi

- 1900—1910

梧州西江沿岸侯莱克修道院 > The Hou Lik Monastery on the bank of the Xi River in Wuzhou

广西 — Guangxi

1900年—1910年 — 1900—1910

船楼内 > Inside the house on deck

广西 — Guangxi

1900年—1910年 — 1900—1910

梧州喊着号子的船工们　　>　Boatmen singing the work song in Wuzhou

广西　　　　　　　　　　-　Guangxi

1900年 — 1910年　　　　-　1900—1910

河渠岸上的木材加工厂 > The timber processing plant on the river bank

广西 — Guangxi

1900年—1910年 — 1900—1910

| 梧州的僧侣 | > | Monks in Wuzhou |

| 广西 | – | Guangxi |

| 1900年—1910年 | – | 1900—1910 |

梧州正在水池中浸泡消暑的水牛和树下的牧者 > Buffaloes soaking in the pond and the shepherd under the tree in Wuzhou

广西 - Guangxi

1900年—1910年 - 1900—1910

我们到达梧州后,在岸上等待主持者的到达(原图注) > We are waiting for the host on the bank after arriving at Wuzhou.

广西 — Guangxi

1900年 — 1910年 — 1900—1910

西江梧州附近，沿河岸建有很多高脚房子 > Along the river bank near Wuzhou on the Xi River locates many high buildings

广西 — Guangxi

1900年—1910年 — 1900—1910

西江梧州附近，沿河岸建有很多高脚房子 > Along the river bank near Wuzhou on the Xi River locates many high buildings

沿梧州西江河岸建的高脚房子　>　High buildings on the bank of the Xi River in Wuzhou

广西　—　Guangxi

1900年—1910年　—　1900—1910

沿梧州西江河岸建的高脚房子　>　High buildings on the bank of the Xi River in Wuzhou

广西　—　Guangxi

1900年—1910年　—　1900—1910

梧州西江河面，河对岸的山峦，河中的船只　>　Surface of the Xi River in Wuzhou, mountains on
the other side of the river, boats floating on the river

广西 — Guangxi

1900 — 1910 — 1900—1910

梧州西江河面，对岸的小山丘　>　Surface of the Xi River in Wuzhou, small hills on the opposite bank

广西 — Guangxi

1900 — 1910 — 1900—1910

梧州天后宫牌楼　>　Memorial archway of the Tianhou Temple in Wuzhou

广西　–　Guangxi

1900年 — 1910年　–　1900—1910

梧州农夫正在用水牛犁田　　>　　A farmer is plowing with the buffalo in Wuzhou.

广西　　—　　Guangxi

1900年—1910年　　—　　1900—1910

梧州西江的田园景象　　> 　Idyllic scenery on the Xi River in Wuzhou

广西　　　　　　　　－　Guangxi

1900年 — 1910年　　　－　1900 — 1910

梧州英国领事馆门前 > In front of the British Consulate in Wuzhou

广西 — Guangxi

1900年—1910年 — 1900—1910

梧州路边的景象：山脚下的水田和田间的水牛　　Scenery along the roads in Wuzhou, paddy field at the mountain foot and the buffaloes in the field

广西　　Guangxi

1900年 — 1910年　　1900—1910

全景显示外滩中心的日俄中国银行大楼 > Panorama of the building of Japanese—Russian Bank of China in the Bund center

上海 - Shanghai

1906年—1908年 - 1906—1908

外滩全景 > Panorama of the Bund

上海 — Shanghai

1906年—1908年 — 1906—1908

沿外滩向北的货运码头，江中停满了各式船只 > The shipping dock in the north of the Bund, various kinds of boats berthing on the river

上海 - Shanghai

1906年—1908年 - 1906—1908

街头的商贩和人群　>　Vendors and crowds on the street

上海　—　Shanghai

1906年—1908年　—　1906—1908

日俄中国银行大厦，门前停着许多候客的人力车 > The building of Japanese—Russian Bank of China, many rickshaws waiting for guests in front of the gate

上海 — Shanghai

1906年—1908年 — 1906—1908

一条商业街，两边店肆林立 > A business street with stores standing alongside

上海 — Shanghai

1906年—1908年 — 1906—1908

五层骑楼和街景，街角处是候客的人力车

上海

1906年—1908年

A five-floor arcade and the street scenery, rickshaws waiting for guests in the corner

Shanghai

1906—1908

维多利亚风格建筑，拉着客人奔跑在大街上的人力车

上海

1906年—1908年

Building of Victoria style, rickshaws carrying guests on the street

Shanghai

1906—1908

两座维多利亚风格的建筑，外滩路口 > Two sets of buildings of Victoria style on the crossing of the Bund

上海 — Shanghai

1906年—1908年 — 1906—1908

四层骑楼建筑	>	A four-storey arcade
上海	–	Shanghai
1906年 — 1908年	–	1906 — 1908

繁忙的江面,沿江北望,远处是一个大的仓库　>　Busy people on the river. Viewing the north along the river, there is a big warehouse in the distance.

上海　—　Shanghai

1906年—1908年　—　1906—1908

停泊在黄浦江里的轮船 > Ships berthing at the Huangpu River

上海 — Shanghai

1906年—1908年 — 1906—1908

失火被焚毁的汉口轮（S.S. Hankow）	>	S.S. Hankow destroyed by fire
上海	-	Shanghai
1906年 — 1908年	-	1906 — 1908

舢板在外滩北的江面上一字排开 > Sampans lining up on the river in the north of the Bund

上海 - Shanghai

1906年—1908年 - 1906—1908

苏州河上的太古码头和巴特菲尔德号轮 > Taiku dock and Butterfield cruise on the Suzhou River

上海 - Shanghai

1906年—1908年 - 1906—1908

苏州河上的舢板和蒸汽轮　>　Sampans and a steam ship on the Suzhou River

上海　　　　　　　　　　　-　Shanghai

1906年—1908年　　　　　　-　1906—1908

苏州河上的舢板 > Sampans on the Suzhou River

上海 — Shanghai

1906年—1908年 — 1906—1908

苏州河上繁华景像，远处是花园大桥 > Prosperous scene on the Suzhou River, with garden bridge in the distance

上海 — Shanghai

1906年—1908年 — 1906—1908

横跨苏州河的石拱桥	>	Stone arch bridge crossing the Suzhou River
上海	—	Shanghai
1906年—1908年	—	1906—1908

中国式拱桥	>	Chinese style arch bridge
上海	—	Shanghai
1906年—1908年	—	1906—1908

走在运河岸上的中国军队 > Chinese army marching along the bank of the canal

上海 — Shanghai

1906年—1908年 — 1906—1908

稻田中的一座高大宝塔 > A tall tower in the paddy field

上海 — Shanghai

1906年 — 1908年 — 1906—1908

从江中远望建在城墙一角的庙宇 > Viewing the temples in the corner of the city wall from the river

上海 — Shanghai

1906年—1908年 — 1906—1908

九江火车站，列车刚刚从南京抵达 > Jiujiang Train Station, the train is just arriving from Nanjing.

江西 — Jiangxi

1907年—1908年 — 1907—1908

沿汉口长江的城墙 > City walls along the bank of the Yangtze River in Hankou

湖北 — Hubei

1906年—1908年 — 1906—1908

在上海至汉口的船上，远处江心岛上，坐落着一个庙宇 > On the ship from Shanghai to Hankou, a temple is located on the island in the center of the distant river.

湖北 — Hubei

1906年—1908年 — 1906—1908

汉口长江边的建筑 > Buildings along the Yangtze River in Hankou

湖北 — Hubei

1906年—1908年 — 1906—1908

汉口长江上的帆船 > Sailing boats on the Yangtze River in Hankou

湖北 — Hubei

1906年—1908年 — 1906—1908

| 在上海至汉口的船上，运木材的木排伐顺流而下 | > | On the ship from Shanghai to Hankou, rafts shipping wood are floating downstream. |

湖北 — Hubei

1906年—1908年 — 1906—1908

上海至汉口的途中,中国军队排列在长江岸边,有些人还骑着驴子 > On the way from Shanghai to Hankou, Chinese army are lining up along the bank of the Yangtze River, and some people are riding donkeys.

湖北 — Hubei

1906年—1908年 — 1906—1908

汉口舢板上的中国男子 > Chinese men on the sampan in HanKou

湖北 — Hubei

1906年—1908年 — 1906—1908

宽阔的汉口长江江面和江上的白布帆船 > The broad Yangtze River in Hankou and white cloth sailing boats on the river

湖北 — Hubei

1906年 — 1908年 — 1906—1908

汉口长江沿岸全景：梯田与城墙 > Panorama of the bank of the Yangtze River in Hankou: terrace and city walls

湖北 — Hubei

1906年 — 1908年 — 1906—1908

汉口长江沿岸全景照片：梯田与湖泊 > Panorama of the bank of the Yangtze River in Hankou: terrace and lakes

湖北 — Hubei

1906年—1908年 — 1906—1908

| 汉口长江，外城门入口 | > | The Yangtze River in Hankou, the entrance of the outer city gate |

湖北 — Hubei

1906年 — 1908年 — 1906—1908

| 汉口长江与远处的城墙 | > | The Yangtze River in Hankou and the city walls in the distance |

湖北 — Hubei

1906年 — 1908年 — 1906—1908

位于汉口的赫明斯和巴克利的办公室 > Hemmings and Berkley's offices located in Hankou

湖北 — Hubei

1914年 — 1914

前门	>	The front gate
北京	—	Beijing
1900年—1910年	—	1900—1910

北京石舫,又叫清晏舫,位于昆明湖西北,万寿山西麓岸边。建于清乾隆二十年(1755年)

> The Beijing Marble Boat, also named Qingyan Boat, which is located in the northwest of the Kunming Lake, the west bank of the foot of the Wanshou Mountain, built in the 20th year during the reign of Emperor Qianlong(1755).

北京 — Beijing

1906年 — 1909年 — 1906—1909

天坛圜丘一角　　　>　A corner of Circular Mound Altar in Temple of Heaven

北京　　　　　　　—　Beijing

1906年—1908年　　—　1906—1908

潭柘寺庭院内的古树与建筑 > An old tree and houses in the courtyard of Tanzhe Temple

北京 — Beijing

1912年 — 1912

潭柘寺院落一角的古树 > An old tree in the corner of the courtyard of Tanzhe Temple

北京 — Beijing

1912年 — 1912

潭柘寺庭院内的香炉 > The incense burner in the courtyard of Tanzhe Temple

北京 — Beijing

1912年 — 1912

| 高处望潭柘寺建筑群落的宇顶 | > | Aerial view of the top of the buildings in Tanzhe Temple |

北京 — Beijing

1912年 — 1912

群山环抱中的潭柘寺	>	Tanzhe Temple surrounded by mountains
北京	—	Beijing
1912年	—	1912

潭柘寺的塔林　>　Tower and trees in Tanzhe Temple

北京　—　Beijing

1912年　—　1912

一座村庄的入口 > The entrance of a village

北京 — Beijing

1906年—1908年 — 1906—1908

一座村庄的入口旁的树木 / Trees beside the entrance of a village

北京 / Beijing

1906 — 1908

古北口，运载货物的骡车与驼队 > Gubeikou, mules and camel teams carrying goods

热河 — Jehol

1909年5月8日 — 1909.5.8

古北口，河谷与长城 > Gubeikou, the river valley and the Great Wall

热河 — Jehol

1909年5月8日 — 1909.5.8

古北口，山顶上的长城	>	Gubeikou, the Great Wall on the mountain top
热河	–	Jehol
1909年5月8日	–	1909.5.8

承德附近的山峦与河谷	>	Mountains and river valleys near Chengde
热河	–	Jehol
1909年5月12日	–	1909.5.12

承德避暑山庄 > Chengde Imperial Summer Resort

热河 — Jehol

1909年5月12日 — 1909.5.12

承德避暑山庄与附近山峦　>　Chengde Imperial Summer Resort and mountains nearby

热河　—　Jehol

1909年5月12日　　1909.5.12

承德避暑山庄 · Chengde Imperial Summer Resort

热河 · Jehol

1909.5.12 · 1909.5.12

承德避暑山庄与附近山岭 > Chengde Imperial Summer Resort and ridges nearby

热河 — Jehol

1909年5月12日 — 1909.5.12

承德鸟瞰 > Aerial view of Chengde

热河 — Jehol

1909年5月13日 — 1909.5.13

承德棒槌山及山下的原野　>　The Bangchui Mountain in Chengde and the plains at the mountain foot

热河　—　Jehol

1909年5月13日　—　1909.5.13

承德的山岭和原野 > Ridges and plains in Chengde

热河 — Jehol

1909年5月13日 — 1909.5.13

承德滦河 > The Luan River in Chengde

热河 — Jehol

1909年5月13日 — 1909.5.13

承德围场，草场和远处的山峰 > Paddock in Chengde, the grassland and the distant peaks

热河 — Jehol

1909年5月18日—1909年6月5日 — 1909.5.18—1909.6.5

承德围场，山峦和谷地 > Mountains and valleys of the paddock in Chengde

热河 — Jehol

1909年5月18日—1909年6月5日 — 1909.5.18—1909.6.5

承德围场，山脚下的村镇 > Paddock in Chengde, villages at the mountain foot

热河 — Jehol

1909年5月18日 — 1909年6月5日 — 1909.5.18 — 1909.6.5

承德围场，山岭中的草丛和林木 > Grass and trees in the ridges of the paddock in Chengde

热河 — Jehol

1909年5月18日 — 1909年6月5日 — 1909.5.18 — 1909.6.5

承德围场，山岭和谷地 > Ridges and valleys of the paddock in Chengde

热河 – Jehol

1909年5月18日 — 1909年6月5日 – 1909.5.18 —1909.6.5

承德围场，山坡上的林木 > Trees on the hillside of the paddock in Chengde

热河 — Jehol

1909年5月18日 — 1909年6月5日 — 1909.5.18—1909.6.5

承德围场,两山之间的谷地草场 > Paddock in Chengde, valley and grassland between two mountains

热河 — Jehol

1909年5月18日 — 1909年6月5日 — 1909.5.18—1909.6.5

承德围场，植被稀疏的山头与草坡 > Paddock in Chengde, sparsely vegetated hill tops and grass slopes

热河 — Jehol

1909年5月18日 — 1909年6月5日 — 1909.5.18 — 1909.6.5

承德围场，山坡上的树木 > Paddock in Chengde, trees on the hillside

热河 — Jehol

1909年5月18日 — 1909年6月5日 — 1909.5.18 — 1909.6.5

承德围场，山岭草坡 > Paddock in Chengde, ridges and grass slopes

热河 — Jehol

1909年5月18日 — 1909年6月5日 — 1909.5.18 — 1909.6.5

承德围场，山岭草坡 > Paddock in Chengde, ridges and grass slopes

热河 — Jehol

1909年5月18日 — 1909年6月5日   1909.5.18 — 1909.6.5

承德围场，谷地草场与河流 > Paddock in Chengde, valley, grassland and rivers

热河 — Jehol

1909年5月18日 — 1909年6月5日 — 1909.5.18—1909.6.5

承德围场,锥子山下的村落与草场 > Paddock in Chengde, the villages and grassland under the Zhuizi Mountain

热河 — Jehol

1909年5月18日—1909年6月5日 — 1909.5.18—1909.6.5

承德围场，锥子山下依山而建的村落营地 > Paddock in Chengde, village campsites built along the foot of the Zhuizi Mountain

热河 — Jehol

1909年5月18日——1909年6月5日 — 1909.5.18—1909.6.5

承德围场，锥子山山峰与山下草场 > Paddock in Chengde, peaks of the Zhuizi Mountain and the grassland at the mountain foot

热河 — Jehol

1909年5月18日 — 1909年6月5日 — 1909.5.18 — 1909.6.5

承德围场，村民与孩子们 > Paddock in Chengde, villagers and children

热河 – Jehol

1909年6月6日—1909年6月18日 – 1909.6.6—1909.6.18

承德围场，载货的马队 > Paddock in Chengde, the horse team carrying goods

热河 — Jehol

1909年7月 — 1909.7

承德围场，草场与屋舍 > Paddock in Chengde, grassland and cottages

热河 — Jehol

1909年7月 — 1909.7

承德围场，宽阔的草场　>　Paddock in Chengde, the broad grassland

热河　—　Jehol

1909年7月　—　1909.7

承德围场，平坦的谷地 > Paddock in Chengde, the flat valley

热河 — Jehol

1909年7月 — 1909.7

承德围场，湖泊 > Paddock in Chengde, the lake

热河 — Jehol

1909年7月 — 1909.7

承德围场，草场上的小河   >   Paddock in Chengde, a small river on the grassland

热河   —   Jehol

1909年7月   —   1909.7

承德围场，山谷草场上的道路与骑车的人 > Paddock in Chengde, the path on the grassland of the valley and the people riding the horse

热河 — Jehol

1909年7月 — 1909.7

承德围场，山峦与谷地 > Paddock in Chengde, mountains and valleys

热河 — Jehol

1909年7月 — 1909.7

承德围场，山坡上的林木与草丛　　Paddock in Chengde, trees and grass on the hill slope

承德围场，三道沟（音，Santago） > Paddock in Chengde, Santago

热河 — Jehol

1909年7月 — 1909.7

承德围场的妇女 > A woman on paddock in Chengde

热河 — Jehol

1909年7月 — 1909.7

承德围场的力士 > Hercules on paddock in Chengde

热河 — Jehol

1909年7月 — 1909.7

承德围场的清军车队 > Horse team of Qing army on paddock in Chengde

热河 — Jehol

1909年7月 — 1909.7

承德围场接受检阅的军队与围观的人群　>　Paddock in Chengde, the army in inspection and the onlooking crowd

热河　—　Jehol

1909年8月　—　1909.8

五台山塔院寺 > Tayuan Temple on Wutai Mountain

山西 — Shanxi

1909年9月 — 1909.9

五台山山岭与塔院寺 > Wutai Mountain, ridges and Tayuan Temple

山西 — Shanxi

1909年9月 — 1909.9

五台山山谷中的塔院寺 > Wutai Mountain, Tayuan Temple in the valley

山西 — Shanxi

1909年9月 — 1909.9

五台山的梯田与山村 > Wutai Mountain, terrace and villages

山西 — Shanxi

1909年9月 — 1909.9

岷县屋宇与道路　>　Houses and roads in the Min County

甘肃　　　　　　—　Gansu

1911年5月　　　—　1911.5

从四川来的商人与背着货物的劳力 > Businessmen from Sichuan and labors carrying goods

甘肃 — Gansu

1911年5月 — 1911.5

回族士兵 > Soldiers of the Hui nationality

甘肃 — Gansu

1911年6月 — 1911.6

洮河上的木桥 > The wooden bridge over the Tao River

甘肃 — Gansu

1911年6月 — 1911.6

洮河上的木桥　>　The wooden bridge over the Tao River

甘肃　—　Gansu

1911年6月　—　1911.6

柳林的背夫，倚在墙边等着活计　>　Porters in Liulin leaning on the wall and waiting for work

甘肃　—　Gansu

1911年6月　—　1911.6

柳林的村落，坐落于山坡谷地之间 > Villages in Liulin, which is located between hills and valleys

甘肃 — Gansu

1911年6月 — 1911.6

柳林的儿童 > Children in Liulin

甘肃 — Gansu

1911年6月 — 1911.6

柳林的妇女 > Women in Liulin

甘肃 — Gansu

1911年6月 — 1911.6

柳林的吹号手	>	Trumpeters in Liulin
甘肃	–	Gansu
1911年7月	–	1911.7

洮河河谷 > Valley of the Tao River

甘肃 — Gansu

1911年6月 — 1911.6

柳林的寺庙的法事和众多的围观者	>	Religious rituals in the temple in Liulin and many viewers
甘肃	–	Gansu
1911年7月	–	1911.7

柳林的寺庙的法事和围观的民众　>　Religious rituals in the temple in Liulin and the viewers

甘肃　—　Gansu

1911年7月　—　1911.7

柳林的寺庙的法事仪式 > Religious ceremony in the temple in Liulin

甘肃 — Gansu

1911年7月 — 1911.7

柳林的寺庙正在举行法事 > Temple in Liulin is hosting the religious rituals

甘肃 — Gansu

1911 年 7 月 — 1911.7

柳林寺庙法事的热闹场面 > Lively scene of religious ceremony in the temple in Liulin

甘肃 — Gansu

1911年7月 — 1911.7

柳林寺庙法事仪式 > Religious ceremony in the temple in Liulin

甘肃 — Gansu

1911年7月 — 1911.7

柳林的塔 > The pagoda in Liulin

甘肃 – Gansu

1911年7月 – 1911.7

柳林寺庙的法事 > Religious rituals in the temple in Liulin

藏族妇女装束 > The attire of a Tibetan woman

甘肃 — Gansu

1911年7月9日 — 1911.7.9

| 藏族姑娘 | > | A Tibetan girl | | 藏族一家 | > | A Tibetan family |

| 甘肃 | − | Gansu | | 甘肃 | − | Gansu |

| 1911年7月9日 | − | 1911.7.9 | | 1911年7月9日 | − | 1911.7.9 |

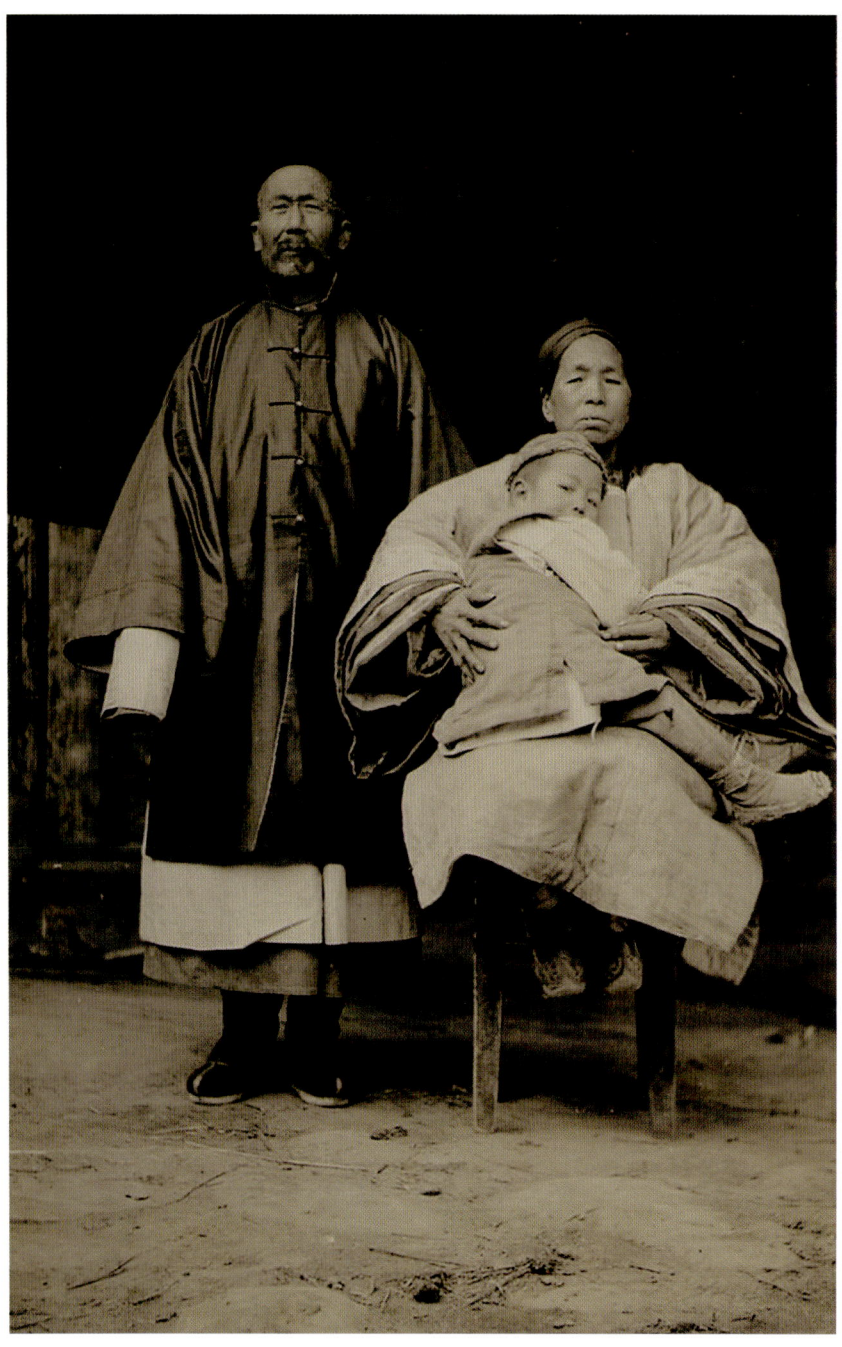

洮河河谷穿官服的的藏族一家 > A Tibetan family on robes in the valley of the Tao River

甘肃 — Gansu

1911年7月9日 — 1911.7.9

洮河河谷的藏族僧人 > A Tibetan buddhist in the valley of the Tao River

甘肃 — Gansu

1911年7月9日 — 1911.7.9

洮河河谷的藏族罗伯（音，Robber）酋长　>　Robber, Tibetan tribal chief in the valley of the Tao River

甘肃　—　Gansu

1911年7月9日　—　1911.7.9

洮河河谷的藏族罗伯（音，Robber）酋长　Robber, Tibetan tribal chief in the valley of the Tao River

甘肃　—　Gansu

1911年7月9日　—　1911.7.9

洮河河谷的藏族老人与青年男子 > Old and young Tibetan men in the valley of the Tao River

甘肃 — Gansu

1911年7月9日 — 1911.7.9

洮河河谷的藏族罗伯（音，Robber）酋长戴着帽子站在屋前

甘肃

1911年7月9日

Robber, Tibetan tribal chief in the valley of the Tao River, is standing in front of the house with his hat.

Gansu

1909.7.9

洮河河谷的藏族男子　>　A Tibetan man in the valley of the Tao River

甘肃　—　Gansu

1911年7月9日　—　1911.7.9

洮河附近的藏族寺庙 > The Tibetan temple near the Tao River

甘肃 — Gansu

1911年7月9日 — 1911.7.9

洮河畔的藏族查巴（音，Chapa）村 > The Tibetan Chapa Village on the bank of the Tao River

甘肃 — Gansu

1911年7月9日 — 1911.7.9

洮河河谷的藏族女孩们　>　Tibetan girls in the valley of the Tao River

甘肃　—　Gansu

1911年7月10日　—　1911.7.10

洮河河谷的藏族青年 > Young Tibetan men in the valley of the Tao River

甘肃 — Gansu

1911年7月10日 — 1911.7.10

洮河河谷的长辫子藏族女孩 > A Tibetan girl with a long braid in the valley of the Tao River

甘肃 — Gansu

1911年7月10日 — 1911.7.10

横跨洮河上的木桥 > The wooden bridge over the Tao River

甘肃 — Gansu

1911年7月10日 — 1911.7.10

罗塔尼（音，Lo—ta—ni）附近的桥 > The bridge near Lo—ta—ni

甘肃 — Gansu

1911年8月 — 1911.8

舟曲罗塔尼（音，Lo—ta—ni）附近的木桥 > The wooden bridge near Lo—ta—ni in Zhouqu

甘肃 — Gansu

1911年8月 — 1911.8

舟曲罗塔尼（音，Lo—ta—ni）附近的桥　　>　　The bridge near Lo—ta—ni in Zhouqu

甘肃　　　　　　　　　　　　　　　　　—　　Gansu

1911年8月　　　　　　　　　　　　　　—　　1911.8

洮州（音，Touchow）东北的大山 > Mountains in the northeast of Touchow

甘肃 — Gansu

1911年8月 — 1911.8

临潭的藏族妇女 > Tibetan women in Lintan

甘肃 — Gansu

1911年8月10日 — 1911.8.10

临潭的藏族男子 > A Tibetan man in Lintan

甘肃 — Gansu

1911年8月10日 — 1911.8.10

临潭山坡上的藏族帐篷 > Tibetan tents on the hill in Lintan

甘肃 — Gansu

1911年8月10日 — 1911.8.10

流经临潭境内的洮河和两岸的坡地、山岭 > The Tao River flowing through Lintan and the slopes and ridges along banks

甘肃 — Gansu

1911年8月10日 — 1911.8.10

西青山（音，Xiqing Shan）	>	Xiqing Shan
甘肃	–	Gansu
1911年9月	–	1911.9

西青山（音，Xiqing Shan） > Xiqing Shan

甘肃 — Gansu

1911年9月 — 1911.9

入山的寨口 > The village entrance to the mountain

甘肃 — Gansu

1911年10月12日 — 1911.10.12

洮河的水流与岸上坡地上生长的矮木丛 > Flow of the Tao River and bushes growing on the slope of the bank

甘肃 - Gansu

1911年10月12日 - 1911.10.12

洮河河流和岸上的小亭 > The Tao River and a small pavilion on the bank

甘肃 — Gansu

1911年10月12日 — 1911.10.12

北岭（音，Peling）境内的峡谷 > Gorges in Peling

甘肃 — Gansu

1911年11月 — 1911.11